SOME MAJOR EVENTS IN WORLD WAR II

THE EUROPEAN THEATER

1939 SEPTEMBER—Germany invades Poland; Great Britain, France, Australia, & New Zealand declare war on Germany; Battle of the Atlantic begins. NOVEMBER—Russia invades Finland.

1940 APRIL—Germany invades Denmark & Norway. MAY—Germany invades Belgium, Luxembourg, & The Netherlands; British forces retreat to Dunkirk and escape to England. JUNE—Italy declares war on Britain & France; France surrenders to Germany. JULY—Battle of Britain begins. SEPTEMBER—Italy invades Egypt; Germany, Italy, & Japan form the Axis countries. OCTOBER—Italy invades Greece. NOVEMBER—Battle of Britain over. DECEMBER—Britain attacks Italy in North Africa.

1941 JANUARY—Allies take Tobruk. FEBRUARY—Rommel arrives at Tripoli. APRIL—Germany invades Greece & Yugoslavia. JUNE—Allies are in Syria; Germany invades Russia. JULY—Russia joins Allies. AUGUST—Germans capture Kiev. OCTOBER—Germany reaches Moscow. DECEMBER—Germans retreat from Moscow; Japan attacks Pearl Harbor; United States enters war against Axis nations.

1942 MAY—first British bomber attack on Cologne. JUNE—Germans take Tobruk. SEPTEMBER—Battle of Stalingrad begins. OCTOBER—Battle of El Alamein begins. NOVEMBER—Allies recapture Tobruk; Russians counterattack at Stalingrad.

1943 JANUARY—Allies take Tripoli. FEBRUARY—German troops at Stalingrad surrender. APRIL—revolt of Warsaw Ghetto Jews begins. MAY—German and Italian resistance in North Africa is over; their troops surrender in Tunisia; Warsaw Ghetto revolt is put down by Germany. JULY—allies invade Sicily; Mussolini put in prison. SEPTEMBER—Allies land in Italy; Italians surrender; Germans occupy Rome; Mussolini rescued by Germany. OCTOBER—Allies capture Naples; Italy declares war on Germany. NOVEMBER—Russians recapture Kiev.

1944 JANUARY—Allies land at Anzio. JUNE—Rome falls to Allies; Allies land in Normandy (D-Day). JULY—assassination attempt on Hitler fails. AUGUST—Allies land in southern France. SEPTEMBER—Brussels freed. OCTOBER—Athens liberated. DECEMBER—Battle of the Bulge.

1945 JANUARY—Russians free Warsaw. FEBRUARY—Dresden bombed. APRIL—Americans take Belsen and Buchenwald concentration camps; Russians free Vienna; Russians take over Berlin; Mussolini killed; Hitler commits suicide. MAY—Germany surrenders; Goering captured.

THE PACIFIC THEATER

1940 SEPTEMBER—Japan joins Axis nations Germany & Italy.

1941 APRIL—Russia & Japan sign neutrality pact. DECEMBER—Japanese launch attacks against Pearl Harbor, Hong Kong, the Philippines, & Malaya; United States and Allied nations declare war on Japan; China declares war on Japan, Germany, & Italy; Japan takes over Guam, Wake Island, & Hong Kong; Japan attacks Burma.

1942 JANUARY—Japan takes over Manila; Japan invades Dutch East Indies. FEBRUARY—Japan takes over Singapore; Battle of the Java Sea. APRIL—Japanese overrun Bataan. MAY—Japan takes Mandalay; Allied forces in Philippines surrender to Japan; Japan takes Corregidor; Battle of the Coral Sea. JUNE—Battle of Midway; Japan occupies Aleutian Islands. AUGUST—United States invades Guadalcanal in the Solomon Islands.

1943 FEBRUARY—Guadalcanal taken by U.S. Marines. MARCH—Japanese begin to retreat in China. APRIL—Yamamoto shot down by U.S. Air Force. MAY—U.S. troops take Aleutian Islands back from Japan. JUNE—Allied troops land in New Guinea. NOVEMBER—U.S. Marines invade Bougainville & Tarawa.

1944 FEBRUARY—Truk liberated. JUNE—Saipan attacked by United States. JULY—battle for Guam begins. OCTOBER—U.S. troops invade Philippines; Battle of Leyte Gulf won by Allies.

1945 JANUARY—Luzon taken; Burma Road won back. MARCH—Iwo Jima freed. APRIL—Okinawa attacked by U.S. troops; President Franklin Roosevelt dies; Harry S. Truman becomes president. JUNE—United States takes Okinawa. AUGUST—atomic bomb dropped on Hiroshima; Russia declares war on Japan; atomic bomb dropped on Nagasaki. SEPTEMBER—Japan surrenders.

WORLD AT WAR

Invasion of Sicily

WORLD AT WAR

Invasion of Sicily

By G.C. Skipper

CHILDRENS PRESS, CHICAGO

These Allied transports are only a small part of the mighty armada that churned through the rough water toward Sicily on July 9, 1943.

FRONTISPIECE:
General Bernard L. Montgomery and Lieutenant General George S. Patton look over a map of Sicily.

Library of Congress Cataloging in Publication Data

Skipper, G. C.
  Invasion of Sicily.

  (His World at war)
  SUMMARY: Describes the events of the Allied invasion of Sicily in the summer of 1943, an event that marked the turning point in the war against the Axis powers.
  1. World War, 1939-1945—Campaigns—Italy—Sicily—Juvenile literature. 2. Sicily—History—1870-1945—Juvenile literature. [1. World War, 1939-1945—Campaigns—Italy—Sicily. 2. Sicily—History—1870-1945] I. Title. II. Series.
D763.S5S56   940.54′21   80-27781
ISBN 0-516-04792-2

   3 4 5 6 7 8 9 10 R 91 90 89 88 87 86 85 84

PICTURE CREDITS:
U.S. ARMY PHOTOGRAPH: Cover, pages 4, 9, 10, 13, 14, 17, 21, 23, 25, 27, 28, 33 (bottom), 34 (top), 37, 38, 39, 40, 41, 42 (bottom), 44, 45, 46
NATIONAL ARCHIVES: page 6
UPI: pages 12, 24, 26, 31, 33 (top), 34 (bottom), 36, 42 (top), 43
LEN MEENTS (map): page 18

COVER PHOTO:
Infantrymen advance along a steep Sicilian cliff near Capo Calava.

The ships began to appear over the horizon on July 9, 1943.

They were exactly on time. Some were coming from the Mediterranean, some from England, and some from the United States.

They would meet near the island of Malta, in the Mediterranean Sea. It seemed an unlikely group. There were warships and small landing craft. There were also two types of vessels never seen before: The DUKW (an amphibious truck) and the LST (landing ship, tanks).

Gradually the ships came together. Some flew the flag of the United States. Some flew the colors of Britain. There were even Canadian flags among the splash of colors. All the flags were being whipped by the wind.

When the ships were assembled, they formed one of the greatest armadas ever seen. It was made up of nearly 3,000 ships of all descriptions. Aboard these ships were 160,000 combat-ready troops, 14,000 vehicles from trucks to jeeps, 600 tanks, and 1,800 huge guns.

Only two months had passed since the final Allied victory in Tunisia. Now, all of North Africa was in the hands of the Allies. From Tunisia, it was only a short distance, over the Mediterranean Sea, to the Italian island of Sicily. The Allies had decided to take Sicily.

The United States Seventh Army was commanded by Lieutenant General George S. Patton. The British Eighth Army was commanded by General Bernard L. Montgomery. These two armies were part of the Fifteenth Army Group, directed by General Sir Harold Alexander. This was the team that would control Operation "Husky," the invasion of Sicily. They were ready. The first large-scale amphibious attack against Axis territory during World War II was about to be launched.

But the target—the rocky, triangle-shaped island of Sicily—was not going to be easy to take.

General Dwight D. Eisenhower (below left), Commander in Chief of Allied Forces in the North African theater of war, was in charge of Operation "Husky." Directly under him was General Sir Harold Alexander (left), in charge of the Fifteenth Army Group. This group was made up of the United States Seventh Army, commanded by General George S. Patton (below right) and the British Eighth Army, under General Sir Bernard L. Montgomery (far left, in the beret).

German and Italian soldiers waited for the Allied invasion in these concrete pillboxes near Gela, Sicily, where the American troops were to land.

The island's face was pockmarked with enemy pillboxes. They had been built in depressions that had been blasted out of the rocky ground. Inside the pillboxes waited Italian and German soldiers. There were thirteen enemy divisions on the island—a total of about 400,000 soldiers. About 315,000 of these were Italian and 90,000 were German. All were under the command of Nazi Field Marshal Albert Kesselring.

These soldiers were jumpy and tired. They knew the beaches surrounding the island were covered with coils of barbed wire. But that was not much comfort. The troops were edgy and nervous. They were under terrific strain. Night after night, day after day, they had been on the alert for an invasion. But the invasion hadn't come.

They were also confused. Terrible Allied bombing raids had constantly pounded both Sicily and Sardinia. Which island would be the target of the invasion?

To make matters worse, Allied ships in the Mediterranean were steaming in all directions. Intelligence reports said that many of the ships appeared to be headed toward Greece. None of it made any sense.

American air attacks had wiped out train-ferries in the Strait of Messina (above), so that the enemy could no longer bring food and other supplies from the Italian mainland to Sicily.

One thing did make sense, however. Air attacks had recently become much worse. Four of five German train-ferries had been wiped out in the Strait of Messina. This meant that supplies could no longer be brought from the Italian mainland. Everything was in short supply, including food.

Both the Germans and Italians knew without doubt that an invasion was at hand. They were convinced that the British and Americans would try to come ashore at the western end of Sicily. There, they concentrated their troops—and waited.

But they were wrong.

Before the invasion, Allied air attacks destroyed much valuable enemy equipment. This wrecked plane is in a shattered hangar at Comiso airport.

"I've never seen anything like it," an American soldier said. "Take a look."

The GI next to him was lying down on the deck. "Look at what?" the GI asked.

"Out there. Get up and look," said the soldier.

The GI got slowly to his feet. He had been on the ship for days. He was seasick and didn't want to move at all. But he struggled up and looked beyond the ship's railing.

Troops on the way to Sicily receive last-minute instructions.

For as far as he could see, the water was covered with ships. All kinds of ships. There were big destroyers and tankers and small landing craft. The vessels seemed to stretch out of sight toward the horizon. As the soldier watched, more ships steamed up to join the armada.

"Whadda ya think about that?" asked the soldier.

"Nothing," answered the GI. "The only thing I think is I'm gonna die if I don't get off this boat." With a groan he settled back onto the deck.

The wind picked up suddenly. High above the deck the Stars and Stripes snapped in the wind. The ship bobbed like a cork. It tossed and turned, swayed and dipped.

"Holy cow!" cried the soldier. He looked around. Then he stared up at the dark clouds that had come from nowhere. "There's a storm coming up. We'd better get below."

The GI on the deck pushed back his helmet. "Not me. I don't think I can move. Even if I could, I wouldn't go below. It's like being inside a washing machine down there."

Suddenly there was a sharp clap of thunder. It rumbled across the sky. Bright, harsh legs of lightning danced across the water. Something in the armada was hit. There was a loud bang.

Quickly the GI jumped to his feet. "I can move," he said. "Let's go!"

As the two soldiers ran, the rain started. It lashed down in huge, hard drops that spattered across the deck. Then, just as quickly, it began to come down in torrents. The wind picked up even more. It howled and swirled across the great armada. The ships were knocked around like toys.

Huge ocean swells erupted from the sea. The great warships were tossed around as if they were as light as plywood. The storm raged. The ships dived and tossed, first one way, then the other.

"I'm in the *infantry!* " a soldier shouted. "Get me off this lousy ship!"

"Be glad you ain't a paratrooper!" another soldier yelled back. "The jump boys are gonna go in tonight!"

The cries and complaints of the soldiers faded as they cleared the decks and plunged below.

American and British troops climb down the side of a ship during practice landing maneuvers.

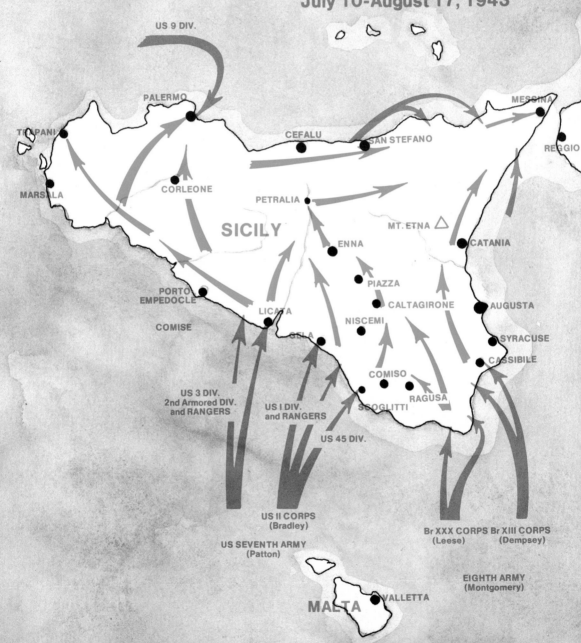

OPERATION "HUSKY"
ALLIED INVASION OF SICILY
July 10-August 17, 1943

US 9 DIV.

PALERMO

MESSINA

TRAPANI

CEFALU

SAN STEFANO

REGGIO

MARSALA

CORLEONE

PETRALIA

MT. ETNA △

CATANIA

SICILY

ENNA

PIAZZA

PORTO
EMPEDOCLE

AUGUSTA

LICATA

CALTAGIRONE

COMISE

NISCEMI

SYRACUSE

GELA

CASSIBILE

COMISO

RAGUSA

SCOGLITTI

US 3 DIV.
2nd Armored DIV.
and RANGERS

US I DIV.
and RANGERS

US 45 DIV.

US II CORPS
(Bradley)

Br XXX CORPS   Br XIII CORPS
(Leese)   (Dempsey)

US SEVENTH ARMY
(Patton)

EIGHTH ARMY
(Montgomery)

VALLETTA

MALTA

In an officer's cabin, the table that held the map was tilted at an angle. The officer quickly grabbed a pencil before it rolled off onto the cabin floor.

"Get me the latest weather reports," the officer said. "We didn't expect a storm."

"Yes, sir!" an aide answered. He picked up the reports and brought them to the officer.

"It's going to be risky if we hit those rocky beaches tomorrow," another officer said.

The first officer continued reading the reports. Then he looked up. "It's a risk we'll have to take," he said. "We're due for better weather soon. But we can't delay the attack."

"Where will the troops go in?" the second officer asked.

"Here," said the first officer. He pointed with the pencil. "Along the southern coast. And here." He moved the pencil on the map. "On the eastern coasts."

"I wonder if the Italians and Nazis know that," said the second officer.

"We'll find out soon enough."

The storm lashed across Sicily's rocky coastline. The rain poured down. A Nazi soldier peered over the top of his pillbox. His head was covered in a slicker. Beyond the beach he could see the ocean. It was pounding against the rocky coast.

The Nazi ducked back down into the pillbox. He sighed with relief. "At least we can sleep tonight," he told his companion. "No army in its right mind would launch an attack in this storm."

About the time the two Nazi soldiers were planning on a good night's sleep, Allied airplanes were roaring off the decks of the carriers in the huge armada.

The American Ninth Division was to land at Palermo (above).

The planes roared through the black, dismal
night toward Sicily. As they approached the island,
they lowered their altitude. The pilots leveled the
aircraft out as much as possible. They flew steadily
through the night.

"Okay, you guys! This is it!"

A door opened. The night wind, cold with rain,
lashed inside the airplane. The first paratrooper
stood at the door. He waited only a moment. Then
he jumped. Quickly, other paratroopers dived out
into the dark sky.

In the wind and the rain, their chutes made little popping sounds as they opened, caught, and yanked upward with a jerk. Then, gradually, the paratroopers glided down toward the dark, dangerous island.

They had orders to meet as soon as possible after landing. Then they were to cut all the communications lines on the island. Other paratroopers would drop at airfields. They had one job to do—move in and take over.

When dawn broke the next morning—July 10, 1943—the sea was still rough. The great armada churned toward Sicily. The order had been given. The invasion of Sicily was on.

German bombers attack a convoy at Gela during the invasion.

The ships steamed forward. They neared
Sicily's coast. Huge guns aboard the ships
boomed. They recoiled like giant rifles. Shells
whistled and screamed and exploded along the
beaches. The landing craft left the larger ships
and moved toward the beaches. They were
carrying combat troops, trucks, jeeps, mortars,
artillery pieces, and tanks.

The landing craft slammed against the wet sand
of the beaches. The traps opened. Soldiers, bogged
down with equipment, slogged their way onto the
beaches.

Aerial view of a Sicily beach at the time of the invasion.

Some dropped immediately, dead from machine-gun fire that erupted from the pillboxes. Others dropped at the water's edge, waited, then jumped up and ran across the beach. Bullets peppered the sand around them. Sometimes a soldier would drop to one knee, firing his rifle.

Patton's American forces landed at Gela, Licata, and Scoglitti, on the southern coast of Sicily. Immediately, they split into two groups. One group ran and fought its way west. The other group plunged toward the center of the island amid a hail of gunfire.

On July 10, 1943, American troops landed at Licata, Sicily, under fire from enemy guns (above). Army pack mules were brought along to help move supplies over the steep and rocky Sicilian terrain (below).

British troops (above) landed on the southeastern coast.

Meanwhile, the British and Canadian troops under Montgomery hit the beaches on the eastern coast. They overran and captured the port of Syracuse.

When the invasion forces hit Sicily that morning there was little resistance. The Italians and Nazis had expected the Allies to attack on the western coastline. By the time these Axis troops realized that the invasion had hit the southern and

Men check a
tank after
landing
on the beach.

eastern coasts, it was too late. The Allied troops
had advanced headlong into the island. They were
able to move swiftly because of the element of
surprise—and because they had an enormous
amount of manpower and equipment.

As the Americans, Canadians, and British
fought their way into Sicily, the Italians sat in
pillboxes watching anxiously.

Some Italians raised their rifles and fired at the
Allied troops cutting their way through the coils of
barbed wire. Others did not fire at all. They did
nothing. The Allied soldiers continued to crawl
and run across the beaches.

First Division infantrymen dig in for a fight near Troina.

The two American soldiers who were aboard
the ship when the storm hit were among those
running across the beach. A sergeant somewhere
was yelling, "Run! Run! Get it moving!" His voice
seemed far away amid the racket of gunfire,
grenades, and mortar shells. But the two American
soldiers heard him. "Let's go!" one of the GIs
cried. He jumped up and ran, crouching, toward
the place where the enemy waited.

His friend was running behind him. He also
crouched as he ran. He hoped he would make it
across the open ground.

The first American soldier dropped suddenly. His friend almost tripped over the first soldier's combat boots and pack. He also dropped.

"You hit?" he cried out.

"No," came the muffled answer. "Over there, see it?"

"Yeah, I see it," his friend answered. "Another pillbox. You know, a guy could get killed in this place."

"Let's go get it. Then we'll make tracks out of here."

The two men jumped up. They sprayed the area around the pillbox with machine-gun fire. Then suddenly they heard the jabber of voices.

They stopped firing. Afraid and cautious, they waited. Soon a head poked up from the pillbox. Then a white handkerchief fluttered wildly.

The two American GIs couldn't believe what they were seeing. An Italian soldier was rising to his full height. His hands were high above his head in surrender.

As more American troops ran up, more Italian soldiers came out of the pillboxes. Their hands were high in the air.

The Italians had had enough of the war. They surrendered quickly.

Other Italians had managed to get away from the horror of the front lines. They ran to their villages. There they changed into civilian clothes and simply disappeared.

"Well, whadda ya know," one American soldier said in surprise.

By then Italian troops were everywhere. All were glad to give themselves up to the American, British, and Canadian soldiers.

All over the island of Sicily the same thing was happening. Italian troops were giving up in huge numbers—as fast as the Allied armies could reach them. They threw down their rifles and willingly followed their captors.

Italian troops smile in relief as they surrender and welcome their captors.

The Allied forces rounded up the prisoners. They made their way into the villages and towns. There another surprise awaited them.

The Allies approached the villages cautiously. They were braced for hard fighting. But they were determined to capture the villages.

"Now we're *really* in for it," the American soldier whispered to his buddy. Ahead of them they could see a small village. It looked almost peaceful.

"You ready?"

"Yeah. Here we go!" shouted the GI.

The two of them, along with the other soldiers, ran into the streets of the village. Their guns were ready to blast away at the first sign of trouble.

Allied soldiers approached Sicilian villages cautiously, braced for hard fighting with Italian and German troops.

There was joy in the streets of Palermo when these Sicilian
civilians greeted the Allied troops who had freed them from the Nazis.

Suddenly the troops stopped dead in their tracks. Instead of running into vicious enemy gunfire, they ran into wild, cheering Sicilians. They lined the streets to greet the Allied armies with flowers and wine. It was a great celebration.

For years, the Sicilians had hated the Nazis who had overrun their country. Now they were free. The Allied troops were cheered and kissed and hugged by villagers all over the island.

But the Nazis were another story. Although the Sicilians surrendered and welcomed the Allied invaders, the Nazis on Sicily had no intention of giving up.

Among the German troops on the island was the Hermann Goering Panzer Division. These were battle-tough soldiers loyal to the Nazi oath. They would die or escape. But they would never surrender.

With the surprise Allied invasion and the surrender of the Italian armies, the Nazis had been forced to withdraw into the mountains. Now they watched from the slopes of Mount Etna.

They watched as the Allied landing boats came onto the beaches. They watched as some American, British, and Canadian soldiers hit the beaches and dropped and died. They watched as others hit the beaches, got up and ran forward, firing and blasting their way into the defense lines.

British troops storm an enemy stronghold at a railway station in eastern Sicily.

Above: General Patton surveys the town of Gela just after American troops had entered. Below: The ruined town after its capture.

Right: This tank, handicapped by the narrow street, is about to meet the enemy in this Sicilian town. Below: Infantrymen advance along a steep cliff near Capo Calava.

Below right: Fighting at night, under makeshift camouflage, these troops throw shells at retreating Italians and Nazis.

Infantrymen and equipment of the Forty-Fifth Division move toward the front for the big push.

The Nazis, high up in the mountains, saw the landing craft bring tanks and jeeps and artillery and soldiers to Sicily. And they waited and watched as the vehicles ran into the bad country. This was land where streams cut the earth deeply. They watched as tanks and jeeps and trucks bogged down. They watched as the Allied leaders discovered the narrow roads. They watched as these narrow roads quickly jammed the flow of traffic. They watched as the invading armies were brought to a crawl.

The rocky, muddy terrain and the narrow roads slowed down the Allies. But it did not stop them. They fought their way from the beaches into the villages and across the island.

Officers of the British and American divisions (above) met and joined forces for the continuing Allied advance toward Messina.

By July 31, 1943, Patton's American troops and Montgomery's British and Canadian forces linked up. They formed a hard, fighting battle line across the entire island—just south of Mount Etna.

Then the Allies turned their attention to the mountains—where the Nazis were.

They went up fighting. Their machine guns, rifles, and flamethrowers were blazing. They went up the mountains with all the strength and energy and manpower they could muster.

The Nazis fought back just as hard. They were just as determined and just as deadly. But the Allies kept coming.

The Nazis backed up the mountains. On the way, they destroyed bridges and roadways. They left a path of destruction in their wake.

But the Allies could not be stopped. Engineers accomplished amazing things in the mountains. They quickly restored roads that led upward.

The retreating Germans destroyed this road (below left), but Allied troops continued to advance. Americans direct artillery fire on the enemy-held town of Troina (below right).

Nazi troops fleeing north to escape Sicily left a path of
destruction in their wake. Above: Third Division troops tug
and push a motocycle over what is left of a narrow mountain
road. Below: One of many destroyed bridges is replaced.

American combat engineers set off a demolition charge to clear a series of enemy roadblocks during the Sicilian campaign.

They reached mountain passes where bridges had been blown. Here they found gaping gorges that seemed to drop into nothingness between high cliffs. But they did not stop. They moved men and equipment up to the very edges of the gorges. Then they went to work. They built trestles that reached across the deep ravines. They built them strong enough to keep the Allied tanks and trucks and ammunition and soldiers moving— upward and around the mountains toward the Nazis.

The retreating Nazis fled across the Strait of Messina (above) to the Italian mainland, which can be seen in the background.

The Nazis could not defeat the invaders—but they did do one thing. They managed to move two thirds of their crack divisions off the island. They hustled them across the Strait of Messina to the Italian mainland. Those troops would be able to fight another day.

But for now, on Sicily, the Allies could not and would not be stopped. By August 17, 1943—only 38 days after the first landings on the beaches—the Allies had taken Messina. They now controlled the entire island. The capture of Sicily had been accomplished.

Above left: The last of the sweep-up in the smoking ruins of Messina. Above right: Lieutenant General George S. Patton praises his troops for the excellent job they did in Sicily.

The invasion had cost the Italians and the Nazis dearly. The way was now open for the invasion and capture of Italy itself. And the Nazis knew they would no longer be able to count on Italian support.

Following the invasion of Sicily, the president of the United States, Franklin Delano Roosevelt, summed up this turning point of World War II. It was, he said, the beginning of the end.

Residents of Agrigento went back about their
business after the town fell to the Allies.

INDEX

Page numbers in boldface type indicate illustrations

About the Author

A native of Alabama, G.C. Skipper has traveled throughout the world, including Jamaica, Haiti, India, Argentina, the Bahamas, and Mexico. He has written several other children's books as well as an adult novel. Mr. Skipper has also published numerous articles in national magazines. He is now working on his second adult novel. Mr. Skipper and his family live in North Wales, Pennsylvania, a suburb of Philadelphia.